T0277287

Happiness

Editorial Director (French edition)
Julie Rouart

Design
Moshi Moshi Studio

Editorial Director (English edition)
Kate Mascaro

Editor
Helen Adedotun

Translation from the French
Kate Robinson

Cover Design
Audrey Sednaoui

Typesetting and Layout Adaptation
Claude-Olivier Four

Proofreading
Nicole Foster

Production
Louisa Hanifi and Marylou Deserson

Color Separation
IGS, L'Isle-d'Espagnac

Printing
Indice, Spain

Originally published in French
as *Le Bonheur c'est les autres:*
Guide de développement collectif

editions.flammarion.com

22 23 24 3 2 1

ISBN: 978-2-08-020694-7

Legal Deposit: 09/2022

Ines de la Fressange

Sophie Gachet · Olga Sekulic

Happiness

THE ART OF TOGETHERNESS

Illustrations by Ines de la Fressange

Flammarion

CONTENTS

Happiness

PREFACE

Life never turns out how you expect it to,
and that's just fine.

These days, visit any bookstore and you'll find shelves lined with self-help guides. But I wonder if it isn't about time we started thinking differently—personally, I find that my relationships with *others* make me a better person. During the pandemic lockdowns, I realized that even though my family is a wonderful source of support, I missed my friends terribly. I'm convinced that we need other people in order to be truly happy, and to have a joyful existence. We live in an era of "me, me, me," in which no selfie is posted without a filter and personal well-being takes precedence over the collective well-being. I like to think that other people are my lifeline, and that friendship is a sound investment. Lately, we have had the leisure to focus on ourselves. Now it's time to concentrate on others.

Don't worry: I'm not interested in playing the know-it-all "celebrity shrink." And while I do believe it's important to take a close look at one's life, I also think that taking a step back is the best way to grasp the bigger picture. But I can tell you for certain that a life without friends is not a life worth living. Studies agree: friendship makes us happier and even supports overall health.

This book reveals all of the ways in which my relationships bring me happiness. Obviously I didn't write it alone; my friends Olga and Sophie reminded me of everything I do to bring joy into my life. Together, we will show you that there is strength in unity, and that we can accomplish more when we work together. Take the advice in this guide—or don't—it's up to you. But remember: be happy—that's the only goal worth achieving.

LONG LIVE LIFE!

"Friendship, like love, requires a lot of effort, attention, and loyalty. More importantly, it requires us to give the very thing that is worth most to us: our time!"

—Catherine Deneuve

For the LOVE of FRIENDS

Friends are the family you choose!

I have a real family that I love very much,
but I also have many friends who are like brothers and sisters to me.
You could call it a "constituted family."

I love animals, so it delights me to know that we humans are "social animals":

OUR HAPPINESS DEPENDS ON OTHERS.

It's scientifically proven: 70 percent of our happiness depends on our relationships with our friends, family, and colleagues. Without other people, our lives would be meaningless.

According to a study by an American university, our relationships with others increase our chances of survival by 50 percent.

I conclude, therefore, that friends are the key to long life!

Allegedly, limited social interaction can be as harmful as smoking fifteen cigarettes a day, and is even worse than not exercising. Pretty scary, huh? But don't worry—luckily, even if you haven't bothered to see your friends in the last few years and you're only now realizing that it might be a problem, the effects of solitude are reversible. Phew!

So let your friends know: "I have to see you, or I'll die!"

Ask

THE RIGHT QUESTIONS

So you want to make friends—great.
But what should you know before gathering a crowd?

1
IS ONE MAN'S HAPPINESS ANOTHER MAN'S SORROW?

There's no reason why you shouldn't keep company with happy people. Still, I would never abandon my unhappy friends; if I can cheer them up, then I'll be happier too. A study by Concordia University in Quebec has proven that friendship protects us from stress and depression—and you don't need a prescription for that!

2
Does like really seek like?

I'll spare you the list of studies demonstrating that friends often have similar genetic traits. Especially since I'm more of an example of "opposites attract": I have friends from all backgrounds, nationalities, and social classes. Actually, I seek friendship with whoever I like!

3

SHOULD YOU BE COMPLETELY HONEST WITH YOUR FRIENDS?

I would like to say, "of course." But can you really tell a friend that you would prefer to stay at home in pajamas, watching the final episode of the latest Netflix show, than go out for sushi at a crowded restaurant? Why can't you just tell her the truth? The right response to her invitation is "Grab some takeout and come watch my show with me!" A friend you can't be honest with is no friend at all.

4

DO "BEST FRIENDS" exist?

I'm not comfortable with the idea of a "best" friend. Obviously, you might get along better with some people than others, but does that make them better? Are your other friends really not as good? Avoid ranking your friends—no one ever talks about having a "second-best" friend.

ULTIMATELY, ALL OF MY FRIENDS ARE MY BEST FRIENDS!

5

SHOULD YOU TALK **POLITICS** WITH YOUR FRIENDS?

You can, on one condition: that you learn to listen and avoid interrupting the other person because you think you know what they're about to say.

Above all, remain calm.

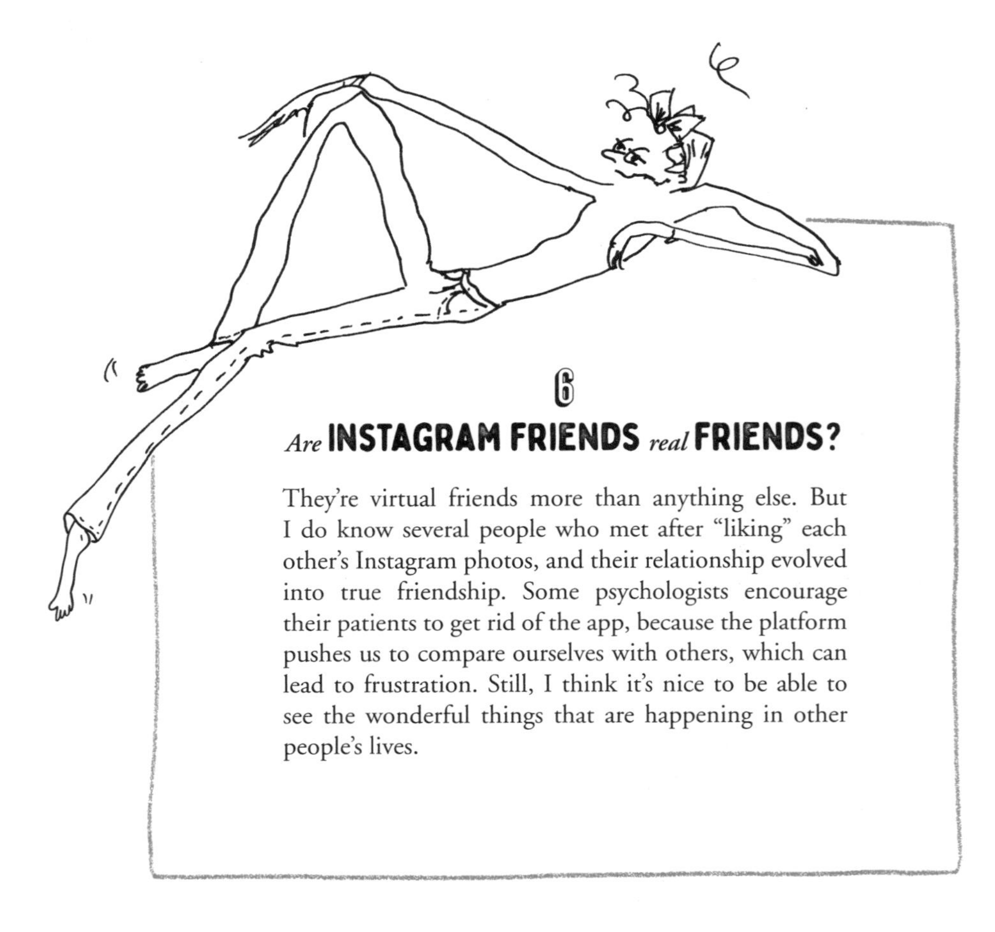

6

Are INSTAGRAM FRIENDS *real* FRIENDS?

They're virtual friends more than anything else. But I do know several people who met after "liking" each other's Instagram photos, and their relationship evolved into true friendship. Some psychologists encourage their patients to get rid of the app, because the platform pushes us to compare ourselves with others, which can lead to frustration. Still, I think it's nice to be able to see the wonderful things that are happening in other people's lives.

If you're too negative, you'll turn people off and you risk alienating your friends one by one. According to American researcher John Cacioppo—one of the founders of social neuroscience—our brains tend to remember negative experiences more readily than positive ones.

LEARN TO FOCUS ON THE POSITIVE.

If you're caught up in negative thoughts, here are a few tips:

Breathe (always good advice).

Avoid people who are negative—and who forget to breathe.

Stand up straight and smile! Smiling stimulates positive thinking. People who don't smile are in no position to be happy. Smile and life will smile back!

Try to push negative thoughts out of your mind. Writing can be a good way to help chase away negativity. Positive thinking leads to a positive view of the world. So instead of saying, "Things are really bad right now. All I've got are problems," try saying, "Life is giving me exciting challenges right now." A change in perspective can make all the difference.

"Don't let a little dispute injure a great friendship."

—Dalai Lama

How do you MAKE FRIENDS?

Childhood and the college years are opportune times for making friends. As an adult, it becomes more difficult to form connections with people you don't know. A friendship isn't built in a day! What can you do to develop friendships? Here are some ideas.

Say THANK YOU

Surely this will come as nothing new—everyone knows that saying thank you is the polite thing to do. Plus, it will make the person on the receiving end want to see you again. Not to mention, the word "gratitude" is very much in fashion at the moment.

CALL *them*

Taking the time to call people and check in on them shows that they are important to you—how can they know if you don't call? It makes sense. "It's the friends you can call up at 4 a.m. that matter," Marlene Dietrich supposedly said.

CELEBRATE *birthdays*

This is so easy to do: just enter your friends' birthdays in an app so you don't forget them. On the big day, give the person a quick call or send a short message—that's all there is to it. If you invite them out to a restaurant or over to your house, surprise them with a cake and candles—they'll consider you their best friend. I know, I know: I just said that all of our friends are our best friends. . . .

SHOW UP *when the going gets rough*

Baptism by fire: this is when you find out who your real friends are. You get divorced, lose your job, or someone close to you dies, and suddenly your "friend" magically disappears. But others will remain very present—even some you didn't expect to. You should be able to share your troubles with your friends. When you can put words to your pain, the burden becomes lighter.

Be **PATIENT**

It's easy to make "friends" on Instagram, TikTok, Snapchat, and Facebook, but forming a solid friendship in the real world takes time: 140 hours to be precise. Jeffrey A. Hall, professor at the University of Kansas, managed to quantify the number of hours of interaction required to form a true friendship with a stranger. Fifty hours is enough to create a friendly relationship, but a deep friendship takes at least 300 hours together. Friends are hard work! I've always known the solution: I'm a very loyal friend.

Tell them they're **IMPORTANT** *to you*

It might seem obvious, but telling your friends that you enjoy spending time with them or that they mean a lot to you really helps form connections. And when someone shows affection, most people try to live up to it. I'm not the only one who believes that you have to be nice in order for people to be nice back: the seventeenth-century philosopher Blaise Pascal said, "Kind words do not cost much, and yet they accomplish much."

Give them **OPPORTUNITIES TO SEE YOU**

Studies have proven that to make friends with someone, they have to be a familiar face. So if you want someone to be your friend, you have to see them often. You'll become a fixture and, as a result, their friend! But you still have to figure out what kind of friend they are—a domesticated canine or an untamed feline—and adjust your behavior accordingly. What type of friend am *I*, you ask? I don't really know, but I do know that I don't shed much.

BRIBE *them*

Yes, giving small gifts can make all the difference. We tend to think that we have to wait for a special occasion to give a gift. But why wait for a commercial holiday when you can spend your money any time you want? It's important for friends to demonstrate small acts of kindness. And if you manage to find a present that suits them perfectly, you'll make their day!

THOUGHTFUL GIFTS FOR FRIENDS

→ a CLUTCH

I'm a "clutchophile," and the extent of my obsession is apparent as soon as you open any of my closets. I have clutch bags everywhere, and I spend my life buying and giving them as gifts.

MY THREE FAVORITES

I can be an extreme minimalist at times. The Golden Eyes clutch by **RSVP** proves that I don't always take the easy option. The two golden rivets on the front look like jeweled eyes.
rsvp-paris.com

Curiosity Lab sells the kind of made-in-India products that I love, and these pouches—each of which is unique—are the perfect example.
curiosity-lab.com

Isaac Reina trained at Hermès, Martin Margiela, and Balenciaga, so it's no wonder this designer's clutches are impeccably simple yet chic. This is a gift you can feel confident giving to anyone.
isaacreina.com

→ *a* CANDLE

A scented candle never fails to please.

MY WAX IDOLS

Bougie 01 (basil, fig leaves, and mint)
by Le Bon Parfumeur
bonparfumeur.com

Jasmin by Diptyque
diptyqueparis.com

Rêve d'Ossian by Oriza L. Le Grand
orizaparfums.com

Japanese candles by Puebco
eu.goodhoodstore.com

Anything from Astier de Villatte
Everything in this store is beautiful, so you really can't go wrong. I want it all—the candles, incense holders, ceramics, and stationery items (especially the Mantes-la-Jolie scented eraser!).
16 Rue de Tournon, Paris 6ᵉ
Tel. +33 (0)1 42 03 43 90
astierdevillatte.com

L'atelier Vime
Located in Vallabrègues, near Avignon, this is one of the most charming houses I've ever visited. It isn't open to the public at the moment, but the objects created there—like these beautiful wicker lampshades—are available on their website. You'll also find vintage furniture for purchase.
International delivery on selected items
ateliervime.com

Dishware by Mr Céramiques
Based in Biarritz, Mélissa Ruffault creates refined, minimalist pieces. Her smooth stoneware plates are superb.
Delivery in Europe only
mrceramiques.com

A notebook by Le Papier
Who's up for a protest? I love notebooks, and those made by Le Papier are emblazoned with the company's slogan: "*Le Papier fait de la résistance*" (Le Papier takes a stand). They're all very beautiful and feature lovely designs, like the one embossed with the words "*Jamais sans mon carnet*" (never without my notebook). Even better, they're all made sustainably in France. Le Papier is only available online though, at
le-papier-fait-de-la-resistance.com

Dishware by
Ines de la Fressange Paris x Yadi
Yes, this is shameless self-promotion, but my coauthors insisted I include this collection. Not least because it is the result of a fruitful collaboration: these unique pieces designed by yours truly were crafted by ceramist Yadi.
Yadi-chic.com
inesdelafressange.fr

Palomas

One day, a delightful young man sent me a box of these meringue-coated pralines. In less than two days, I was completely hooked. These calorie bombs are some of the best candies I've ever had. After gaining a few pounds without realizing it (I only made the connection once the box was empty), I decided that these irresistible treats should be consumed in moderation.

2 Rue du Colonel Chambonnet, 69002 Lyon
Tel. +33 (0)4 78 37 74 60
Delivery in France only
palomas1917.com

Merveilleux cakes

The name says it all—these little treats are "marvelous"! My favorites are from Aux Merveilleux de Fred, where each flavor has a delightful title, such as "L'Incroyable" (The Unbelievable), made of meringue, whipped cream, speculoos cookies, and white chocolate shavings. I like to bring one along when I'm invited to a friend's house for dinner. When I give it to them, I say, "I brought a Merveilleux—it made me think of you."

Stores worldwide
auxmerveilleux.com

Waffles from Méert

The packaging alone is reason enough to buy a box of these dainty sweet treats by the 250-year-old Lille-based pastry maker. You won't find better-tasting waffles than these: created in 1849, they are split in half and filled with Madagascan vanilla cream. They also come in other flavors, some of which are produced in limited editions, just like fashion collections.

*16 Rue Elzévir, Paris 3e*
Tel. +33 (0)1 49 96 56 90
Delivery in Europe only
meert.fr

MÉERT
MÉERT
MÉERT
MÉERT
MÉERT
PÂTES DE FRUITS
COING
9€00 les 100g
PÂTES DE FRUITS
CASSIS
9€00 les 100g
PÂTES DE FRUITS
ABRICOT
9€00 les 100g
PÂTES DE FRUITS
GRIOTTE
9€00 les 100g
GUIMAUVE À
L'ANCIENNE
POIRE
9,00€ les 100g
GUIMAUVE À
L'ANCIENNE
Myrtille
9,00€ les 100g
GUIMAUVE À
L'ANCIENNE
CHOCOLAT
9,00€ les 100g

→ FLOWERS

Ok, it might not be the most original idea, but everyone loves to receive flowers. I know that a bouquet always puts me in a good mood. The real challenge is finding an attractive arrangement.

FOR A GUARANTEED GOOD IMPRESSION

1

Avoid color clashes and choose white flowers.
A white bouquet is never out of place.

2

However, if you dare, it's also fun to mix and match colors to create a country-style posy.

3

If you're lucky enough to have your own garden, homemade arrangements never fail to please!

4

House plants also make a nice gift, especially when presented in a charming pot.

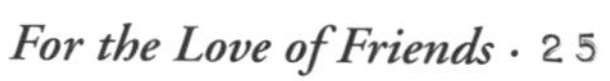

PAULINA 1880

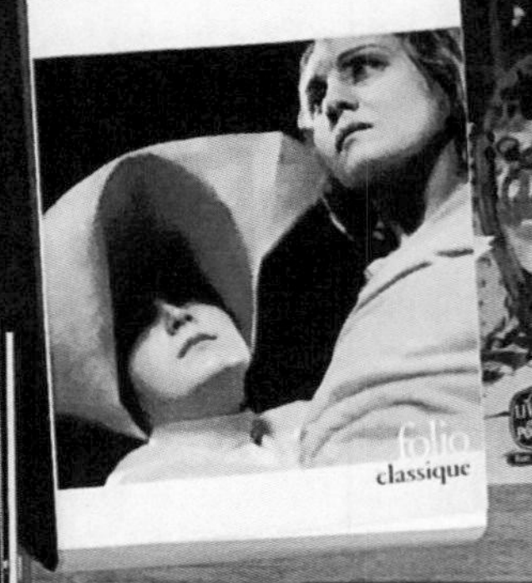
Hugo
Les Misérables I
Édition d'Yves Gohin
folio
classique

Patrick Modiano
Prix Nobel de littérature
Rue des Boutiques Obscures
folio

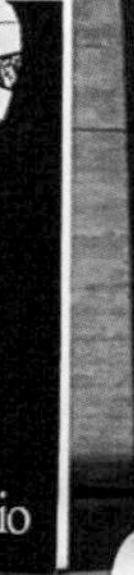
Khalil Gibran
Le Prophète
Préface
d'Amin Maalouf

Joseph
Kessel
rtages, Romans
PRODIGIEUX REPORTAGE
de
JOSEPH KESSEL

Tolstoï
Anna Karénine
Préface de Louis Pauwels
Traduction d'Henri Mongault

Dumas fils
Préface d'André Maurois
Édition de Bernard Raffalli

→ a BOOK

As with wine, it's easy to pick out an award-winning book.
But do you really want to take the easy route? When it comes to friendship,
sometimes it pays to put in the extra effort. So when I give a book as a gift,
I turn to authors who write about friendship.

MY FAVORITES:

On the Road

Jack Kerouac (1957)
Did you know that Kerouac wrote this book in three weeks? A free-spiritedness emanates from this tale of two friends on a journey, up against the whole world.
The famous line: "Our battered suitcases were piled on the sidewalk again; we had longer ways to go. But no matter, the road is life."

•

The Wanderer

Alain-Fournier (1922)
United in tragedy, the three companions in this book
are the very picture of steadfast friendship.
The famous line: "Be my friends in readiness for the day when I shall be again within a hairbreadth of hell, as I have already been. . . . Give me your word that you will come to me if ever you hear me call. . . . You, Meaulnes, swear to it first."

•

The Three Musketeers

Alexandre Dumas (1846)
When it comes to literary friendships, this book is impossible to overlook.
The musketeers stick together through thick and thin.
The famous line: "All for one and one for all!"

The Nicomachean Ethics

Aristotle

This book encourages reflection on happiness and our relationships with others. It teaches us that virtue is essential to life in society and that happiness is the ultimate goal.

The famous line: "Friendship is one soul residing in two bodies."

•

My Brilliant Friend

Elena Ferrante (2012)

Set in working-class Naples, this book follows two friends whose paths cross and diverge. This first volume in the saga begins in post-war Italy and makes for a fascinating read.

The famous line: "If you don't try, nothing ever changes."

Château Lafite: The Almanac

Saskia de Rothschild (2020)

Alright, so this is not a book about friendship—it's a book about wine. But I would give it to any of my friends with pleasure. Drawing on historical archives, anecdotes from daily life at the château, documents, and images by great photographers, the book retraces 150 years of the Rothschild family at Château Lafite. Skillfully put together, it's beautiful, poetic, and funny.

Autobiography of a Yogi

Paramahansa Yogananda (1952)
Steve Jobs, the cofounder of Apple, had time to plan his memorial. His close friends received a gift, into which he slipped a brief note: "Here is Yogananda's book. Actualize yourself." By offering this self-development book, Steve Jobs contributed to

The famous line: "Stillness is the altar of spirit."

SAVE THE DATE

JULY

INTERNATIONAL DAY OF FRIENDSHIP

Initially proclaimed by the United Nations,
this event is serious business.
I think we should all organize dinners
for our friends to celebrate the occasion.
Or take the time to reach out to far-flung friends.

How do you recognize a

true friend?

This is THE question on everyone's mind.
You can't always be sure, but if you answer "yes" to several of these questions, there's a good chance you have a loyal friend.

When chatting with you at a party, do they **MAINTAIN EYE CONTACT** rather than look around for another friend who might be more interesting to talk to?

Do they offer to take care of your plants/ cat/dog/child/mother **WHEN YOU'RE IN A JAM**, even if it means taking a day off work?

Do they **LISTEN ATTENTIVELY** when you tell them that your partner didn't come home last night because they forgot their key and didn't want to wake you?

Can they effortlessly **RESUME A CONVERSATION** from six months ago?

Do they ever say, "I think you're mistaken"?
HONESTY is the key to a successful friendship.
Friends who have our best interests at heart
are worth their weight in gold.

Do they **CALL YOU UP** just because?
And not just to ask a favor.

Do they keep in touch even if you didn't travel
3,000 MILES to attend their birthday party?
(The bank wouldn't loan you the money to pay for the trip.)

Do they turn to you for **SUPPORT**?

The ultimate question:
Is anyone perfect?
Cultivating a less critical
mindset also helps
to attract friends.

Your friend *list*

Sometimes it's a good idea to stop and ask yourself which of your friends you can count on. Who are the ones that matter to you and that are truly part of your life? Review where things stand, and update the guest list for your next birthday party or your holiday card list accordingly—it might sound like a no-brainer, but haven't we all forgotten someone important in the heat of organizing a get-together, or in the holiday rush. While I'm a very loyal friend, the list has been known to change: certain new names appear, but rare is the name that disappears.

I'M A FRIEND
FOR LIFE!

My Talented FRIENDS

My friends understand that I love them simply
for who they are. They enrich my life just by being in it.
I'm proud to say that my friends have talent:
they all have a passion or a profession that defines them.
They, like flowers, bring joy to my life. What are their secrets
to a successful friendship? Here's what they told me.

Vanessa SEWARD,
fashion designer and painter • vanessaseward.com

"I think that tolerance is essential—accepting that we might not always have the same dreams or desires. And accepting that our friends have weaknesses, as well as strengths."

Guillaume HENRY,
artistic director at Patou • patou.com

"A listening ear, laughter, memories, and surprises!"

Marin MONTAGUT,
illustrator-designer • marinmontagut.com

"True friends don't have to see each other often to know that they can always count on one another. Ines and I have been friends for over ten years. We can go months without seeing each other, but we reconnect right away when we meet up again."

Marie-Hélène DE TAILLAC,
jewelry designer • mariehelenedetaillac.com

"My friends are like the precious stones that I work with: they light up my day. We share joy, cheerfulness, and laughter, and they protect me in times of adversity."

Pascale **MONVOISIN,**
jewelry designer • pascalemonvoisin.com

"A friend is someone who knows us by heart. And yet, I think we sometimes take these connections for granted. We must care for them and remember to be considerate and polite, and avoid getting carried away by our own thoughts."

Isabella **ROSSELLINI,**
actress

"Laughter—it makes everything easier. I love laughing with my friends."

Frédéric **PÉRIGOT,**
homeware designer • perigot.fr

"Kindness, discretion, loyalty, and humor, along with a good dose of affection—that's the recipe for a solid friendship!"

Dominique **LIONNET,**
beauty expert • Instagram: @dom_beautytalks

"Is there really a secret or a magic formula for a lasting friendship? I don't know, but if I had to choose one, I'd say be yourself around your friends. Don't invent a character that will be difficult to maintain in the long run."

***Didier* PAPELOUX,**
deputy mayor of Villerville, in Normandy

"Successful friendships are the reward for those who nurture them. Being able to count on each other is the key to true friendship."

***Lilou* FOGLI,**
actress, scriptwriter, and founder of the cosmetics brand Château Berger • chateauberger.com

"To me, friendship is synonymous with trust, sincerity, and loyalty; a desire to share the good times and the bad, and to never feel judged. I like to think that friendship is for life. Ultimately it's a love story—without the sex!"

***Bertrand* BURGALAT,**
musician and producer

"A non-judgmental, trusting relationship."

***Nicole* WISNIAK,**
creator of the magazine *Égoïste*

"Worship your friends' flaws. Tolerate their qualities. Provide unconditional support. Learn to be perceptive and know when to keep quiet."

Bénédicte **PERDRIEL,**
business owner

"Friendship is precious and deserves to be cared for with small kindnesses that technology has made easy: SMS, photos, souvenir-photos (of the best memories), 'hellos,' 'good lucks,' and 'good nights.' We give each other support almost every day."

Alexandre **MATTIUSSI,**
creator of the brand Ami • amiparis.com

"The secret to a successful friendship lies in trust and kindness. Friendship requires that we listen to the other and ask for nothing in return. A sincere friendship is unconditional and for life."

Bernard **CHAPUIS,**
journalist and writer

"If life sends me rain showers, I know Ines will always take me in. And it's been that way ever since we became friends."

Mireille **PELLEN,**
horsewoman

"Tremendous affection. Profound respect. Enormous trust. Sharing a Maresque cocktail while watching the sunset from the terrace of our farmhouse, or by the fire. Chatting, laughing, looking on the bright side—living in the present moment!"

Lydia PUJOLS,
makeup artist

"A successful friendship is one that stands the test of time, that is forged of passion, inspiration, and shared experiences in times of joy and in times of pain. Friendship helps us flourish and move forward in life."

Boris TERRAL,
actor

"As I write the word 'friendship,' I am transported back to a chestnut grove. I wrote this word for the first time on the trunk of a chestnut tree and, next to it, the name of my friend. We must sculpt, carve, and work at friendship."

Héloïse BRION,
cookbook author (*Miss Maggie's Kitchen*) and consultant

"It's the result of a skillful blend of freedom, acceptance, lifelong trust and enduring commitment, differences—in origins, tastes, and opinions—and silences, relaxed and so fulfilling. A successful friendship is the family we choose for ourselves."

Charlotte CHESNAIS,
jewelry designer

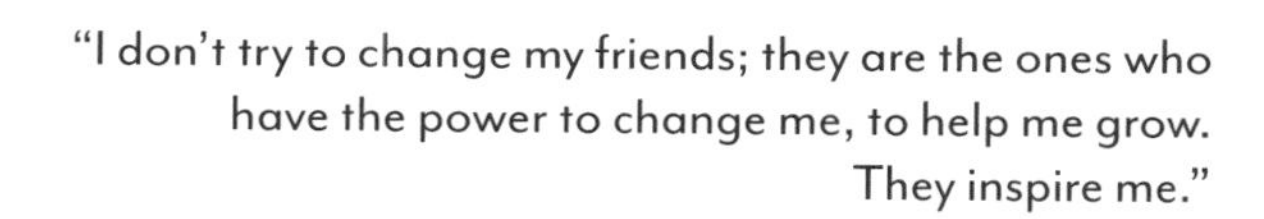

"I don't try to change my friends; they are the ones who have the power to change me, to help me grow. They inspire me."

Andrée ZANA MURAT,
cookbook author

"To be independent and respectful, not intrusive or demanding. To maintain the right distance in order to achieve closeness, not overfamiliarity."

Liya KEBEDE,
top model and designer • lemlem.com

"Loyalty, a listening ear, and camaraderie."

Gilles BENSIMON,
photographer

"For me, friendship is always saying 'yes' before hearing the rest of the question; it's giving everything I've got and accepting both flaws and qualities."

Diego DELLA VALLE,
CEO of Tod's Group

"Without friends or family, life doesn't have much meaning. I've never believed a happy, secure life is possible without deep friendships. Obviously friendship can't be created artificially; it comes from instinct and 'chemistry' between individuals."

***Elie* TOP,**
jewelry designer • elietop.com

"A successful friendship is one that endures beyond the affinities that initially spark the relationship and which form the mortar necessary to build, over time, the house of friendship resting on the pillars of admiration, sharing, respect, steadfastness, attention, and tenderness."

***Vincent* DARRÉ,**
designer and interior architect • maisondarre.com

"Friendship is a playground for unexpected experiences. I like to set off on adventures with my friends. I collect friends, and without them I would die of boredom."

***Delphine* COURTEILLE,**
hairstylist • delphinecourteille.com

"A friendship is like a romantic relationship: both grow and deepen over time and with love. A true, sincere friendship stands the test of time and the trials of everyday life. I might not see certain friends for long periods of time. In those moments, we find ways to maintain our bond."

Fifi **CHACHNIL,**
designer • fifichachnil.paris

"An indescribable feeling of steadfast mutual trust based on a shared vision of life. And recognition."

Marie-France **COHEN,**
founder of the brand Bonpoint and the Paris boutique Merci

"Friends are flowers on the tree of my life, the butterflies and bees that pollinate each and every day."

Cindy **BRUNA,**
model • Instagram: @cindybruna

"Friendship is a two-way relationship that both people invest in and that, like love, must be cared for. It's a choice, so it requires acts of kindness and support."

I THINK IT'S ABSURD
WHEN I HEAR PEOPLE SAY
"I CAN COUNT
MY TRUE FRIENDS
ON JUST ONE HAND."
IN MY CASE, I'D RATHER BE
Shiva.

MOVIES TO CELEBRATE FRIENDSHIP

IT'S A WONDERFUL LIFE

Frank Capra (1946)
After a kind man loses everything, he still has his friends. Just the kind of black-and-white movie I love, starring the handsome James Stewart.
The famous line:
"Remember, George: no man is a failure who has friends. Thanks for the wings! Love, Clarence."

E.T.

Steven Spielberg (1982)
This movie shows how friendship can unite very different individuals. It's also something of an autobiographical film for Spielberg, who didn't have many friends growing up. He was fascinated by UFOs and invented a friend for himself.
The famous line:
"E.T. Phone. Home."

THELMA AND LOUISE

Ridley Scott (1991)
More than a story about friendship, this road movie has become an iconic film for feminists that proves two women united can outmatch violent men. Thirty years after it was made, *Thelma and Louise* is a reference in the "buddy movie" genre.
The famous line:
"Louise, no matter what happens, I'm glad I came with you."

SCARECROW

Jerry Schatzberg (1973)
A film about two losers who hit the road together. Although simple in sentiment, it works—the movie won the Palme d'Or at the Cannes Film Festival in 1973. Al Pacino and Gene Hackman make an irresistibly charming duo.
The famous line:
"You didn't pick me, I picked you."
"Why?"
"Cause you gave me your last match. You made me laugh."

BUTCH CASSIDY AND THE SUNDANCE KID

George Roy Hill (1969)
Two friends are on the run from a sheriff and his posse. This is a western you'll want to watch over and over!
The famous line:
"If I drown, I swear I'll kill you!"

THE HOLE

Jacques Becker (1960)
In prison, Gaspard learns that his fellow inmates have decided to dig a tunnel and escape. He befriends them. This movie was highly acclaimed: French filmmaker François Truffaut called it a masterpiece, and it's one of the greatest French films ever made.
The famous line:
"Poor Gaspard!"

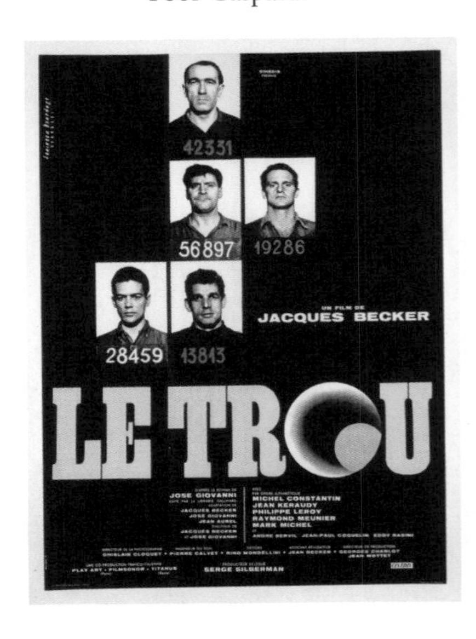

THE GREAT ESCAPE

John Sturges (1963)
Starring Steve McQueen, this movie is based on a true story: in 1943, during World War II, aviators of different nationalities being held in a prison camp dug themselves a tunnel to escape together.
The famous line:
"Wow!"

Real friendship doesn't mean being inseparable; it means you can be separated and nothing changes.

Friendly tunes

"I'll Be There for You"
The Rembrandts (1995),
the theme music from *Friends*

Singing this song is the best way to sum up friendship. The now legendary series is an ode to friends. In each episode, we learn something new about personal relationships. The series gives us the impression that these connections are eternal, much like lessons about friendship. And the cast managed to maintain their camaraderie off-screen.

What did *Friends* teach us about life?

Joey's opinions are often different than everyone else's. So what? That's Joey!

Follow Chandler's lead and always look for the silver lining.

We need to take a leaf out of Phoebe's book and learn not to worry about what others think of us.

No situation is really that serious! You have to take risks and welcome change—that's a characteristic all the *Friends* share. And that's what makes the series so addictive.

Accept your friends as they are: this is the key to the mutual understanding between the cast of *Friends* characters.

"Ain't No Mountain High Enough"
Marvin Gaye and Tammi Terrell (1967)
The message of this song is when you really care about someone, you let nothing stand in your way. If you are separated by distance from your BFF, send them this song—it'll make you feel closer!

♫

"Stand By Me"
Ben E. King (1961)
This song was inspired by the spiritual hymn "Lord Stand By Me." It has since been recorded in more than 400 versions. The theme song of the movie of the same name, it was also featured in a 1987 European commercial for Levi's 501 jeans. It applies equally well to a friend or a romantic partner: the "darlin'" in the lyrics could be anyone.

♫

"With a Little Help from My Friends"
The Beatles (1967)
Just imagine trying to get through life without your ride-or-dies there to support you. Terrifying, right? Clearly, The Beatles knew what was up from day one.

"Lean On Me"

Bill Withers (1972)

In this song, friendship is described as helping us overcome problems. Mary J. Blige performed it in 2009 at Barack Obama's presidential inauguration—it was truly symbolic.

♫

"Wannabe"

Spice Girls (1996)

The Spice Girls knew it best: romantic relationships come and go, but friends are forever. So, if you want to make it work with someone, you have to get along with their friends. The message is clear: if you wanna be their lover, you gotta get with their friends!

♫

"Thank You for Being a Friend"

Andrew Gold (1978)

Best remembered for being the theme song of the sitcom *The Golden Girls*, it's the tune you could send as a gift to your best friend.

♫

"Waiting on a Friend"

The Rolling Stones (1981)

Written by Mick Jagger and Keith Richards, this song talks about the band's friendship—it's legendary, of course!

"Count on Me"
Bruno Mars (2010)
A little like the *Friends* theme song, this one says you can always count on your friends. A simple, basic truth.

"The secret to happiness in love is not being blind,
but knowing when to close your eyes."

—Simone Signoret

LOVE IS in the AIR

The opening quote for this chapter by actress Simone Signoret perfectly encapsulates the secret to a successful romantic relationship: knowing when to overlook the little details that won't matter tomorrow. Ask yourself: did the problem go away overnight, or am I still thinking about it this morning? If sleeping on it did the trick, then it wasn't really a problem to begin with.

In life, you have to learn to let some things go and to turn the page on those things that bring you down.

TAKE STOCK AND FOCUS ONLY ON THE POSITIVE.

LIST 10 POSITIVE things

that you particularly appreciate about your partner.*

* If nothing comes immediately to mind, list 10 annoying things about yourself instead, to remind yourself how lucky you are that your partner loves you regardless!

WHAT IS THE BEST
ANTI-AGING TREATMENT?

Love

The most important thing
is to experience love passionately—
whether it's with a friend, a lover,
or life itself.

WHEN YOU'RE IN LOVE AND SHARING YOUR LIFE WITH SOMEONE, YOU USUALLY MAKE AN EFFORT TO TAKE CARE OF YOURSELF.

THE RESULT: YOU DON'T AGE AS FAST.

But that doesn't mean you're going to die young
if you never find love:
having a zest for life is motivation enough for self-care.

I say this for all of my friends who tell me,
after their divorces,
that they never want to share their life
with another partner again.

WHAT YOU MUSTN'T DO,

under any circumstances,

is let yourself go—or spend every evening
in front of the television eating ice cream
out of the carton.

HOW TO *capture* THEIR HEART

☛ IT'S EASY! According to psychologist Arthur Aron, you can accelerate the process of falling in love by asking the person you're interested in a series of questions. Here's how it works: by asking and responding to personal questions, both individuals feel a shared sense of vulnerability that fosters intimacy.

We haven't tested the method ourselves, but we can tell you that several couples formed as a result of the professor's experiment—and some even got married.

THE TAKEAWAY:
the more we share with our partner, the stronger our relationship will be.

We could have figured that out ourselves, but having these questions in mind might come in handy.

IF I HAD TO REMEMBER ***JUST ONE***, IT WOULD BE:

- Take four minutes and tell your partner your life story in as much detail as possible.

Knowing someone's life story is the best way to find out if you're compatible. A man who doesn't like dogs is automatically eliminated!

Of Dr. Arthur Aron's 36 QUESTIONS, *these are particularly noteworthy:*

They'll add a little spice to your dinner dates.

- Given the choice of anyone in the world, who would you want as a dinner guest?

- What would constitute a "perfect" day for you?

- If you were able to live to the age of 90 and retain either the mind or body of a 30-year-old for the last 60 years of your life, which would you choose?

- What do you feel most grateful for in your life?

- If you could change anything about the way you were raised, what would it be?

- If you could wake up tomorrow having gained any one quality or ability, what would it be?

- What is the greatest accomplishment of your life?

- What is your most treasured memory?

- What is your most terrible memory?

- What does friendship mean to you?

- How close and warm is your family? Do you feel your childhood was happier than most other people's?

- How do you feel about your relationship with your mother?

- Complete this sentence: "I wish I had someone with whom I could share. . . ."

- Tell your partner what you like about them; be very honest this time, saying things that you might not say to someone you've just met.

- When did you last cry in front of another person? By yourself?

- What, if anything, is too serious to be joked about?

- Your house, containing everything you own, catches fire. After saving your loved ones and pets, you have time to safely make a final dash to save one item. What would it be and why?

When you're done with the questions, stare into each other's eyes for four minutes without talking.

And let me know
→ *if you end up tying the knot.* ←

Checklist

Write down your date's qualities (and flaws!), and discuss them together.

DATING IN THE *21st century*

If you haven't yet found your significant other, don't despair—there are a multitude of ways to meet "the one" these days that don't involve cheesy chat-up lines in bars. Social media and apps have revolutionized the dating game.

HOW TO

DECLARE YOUR *love* ON *Instagram*

It's a little clichéd, but a Valentine's Day post is always effective. Just don't be too mushy. You could tease them about one of their little flaws, for instance, but be sure to remind them right away that your love is unconditional.

A simple photo with the words "My ray of sunshine" or "The love of my life" works well, especially if you've had a lot of relationships. It sets the scene for your new life together. I know some very smart guys who opened their Instagram account with a photo of their partner—to start things off on the right foot.

You don't have to be longwinded; a few words is all it takes—and a little humor is always a nice touch. A photo of your sweetheart with the comment "I think they're for keeps" will do the trick.

1

"My ex had incredible self-control. **They ne-ver got mad**."

2

"You've had so many exes. It seems like you were more interested in **quantity than quality**."

3

"That was the best vacation I've ever had. **It's too bad** you couldn't come!"

4

"Have you **put on weight?**"

5

"It's crazy: your brother/sister has all of your qualities but **none of your flaws**."

6

"Did you brush your teeth?"

7

"Did your **gym shut down?**"

8

"I'm so happy summer vacation is over! It was fun, but living together for two weeks, just the two of us—that was a **handful**."

9

"**Who** are you **texting**?"

10

"**My new boss** is incredible: they are attractive, intelligent, **funny—amazing**, in fact. They have everything **going for them**. I haven't met anyone **so perfect in ages**."

10 THINGS TO SAY TO YOUR SWEETHEART AND MAKE THEM WANT YOU FOR LIFE!

♥ "WHAT I LOVE ABOUT YOU IS. . . ." 

Find one or two things that make them stand out.
If you can't, you might want to consider getting a new sweetheart.

"IT'D BE HARD TO FIND A BETTER LOVER THAN YOU."

"I'M NOT IN A HURRY TO SETTLE DOWN."

Their desire to win your heart will change your mind.

EVERYONE LOVES A CHALLENGE.

Be careful, though: this only works with people who really aren't in a hurry to settle down. It can have the opposite effect on hopeless romantics.

"YOU HAVE INCREDIBLE EYES."

 THIS ALWAYS DOES THE TRICK. 

"DID YOU LOSE WEIGHT?"

EVEN IF THAT BEER BELLY IS STARTING TO SHOW.

"LET'S HAVE **DINNER** AT YOUR **MOTHER'S** HOUSE."

"I HAD NO **idea** WHAT **happiness** WAS UNTIL **I met you**."

"I'M SO LUCKY TO HAVE MET YOU."

"HOW DO YOU MANAGE TO LOOK STYLISH IN **FLIP-FLOPS**?"

"Your intelligence should be considered a public service."

→ *Romantic* GIFTS

Choosing a gift for your sweetheart can be a veritable obstacle course. More than just an object, your offering speaks volumes about the way you view your other half. So, avoid household appliances at all costs! Imagine what your beloved would love to receive most in the world, and add a little note to make it more meaningful.

The Home Edit Life: The No-Guilt Guide to Owning What You Want and Organizing Everything
by Clea Shearer and Joanna Teplin
Ok, so don't buy this book if your partner's pet peeve is tidying up. But for those who like their things to be neat and orderly, this playful volume is perfect, and will allow them to organize their home beautifully. Once you start to follow the authors' guidelines, you'll be hooked.
The note: "To ensure our love nest is always shipshape"
thehomeedit.com

TableTopics Couples: Questions to Start Great Conversations
"What's the most romantic thing your partner has done for you?" "If we could quit our jobs what would we like to do?" Find out more about the love of your life and your relationship by posing questions like these from the 135 question cards in the set. An entertaining way to spend a rainy evening.
The note: "Let's get to know each other even better"
tabletopics.com

Polaroid Go
The more senior among us remember the instant camera well. It was very popular in the pre-digital era, as it allowed you to obtain your photo as soon as it was taken. Today, smartphones have largely replaced cameras, but even the young and hip like to be able to pin *real* photos on their wall right away. This new Polaroid camera is compact and easy to carry around.
The note: "To immortalize our love"
polaroid.com

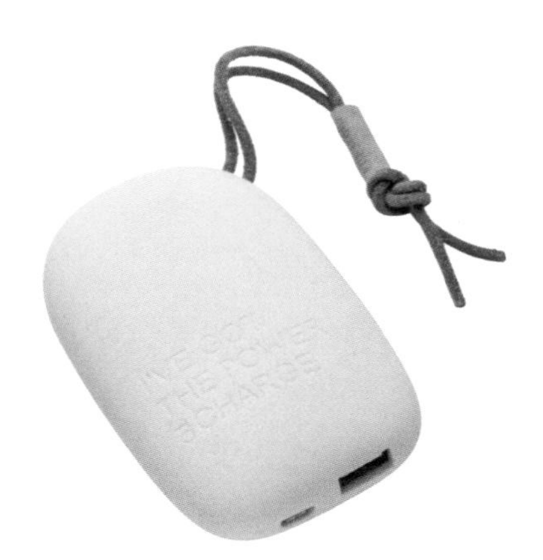

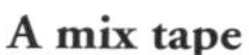

A mix tape
Make your partner an old-fashioned mix tape—whether a playlist or an actual cassette, select an hour of music (around 20 songs) that is meaningful to the two of you: songs that remind you of how you met, a trip you took together, a private joke, or "your song." Extra points if you add one from a band that your partner loves but drives you crazy—just to show that you really *do* pay attention.
The note:
"Listen to the music of our love"

Kreafunk phone charger
More than a simple charger, Kreafunk's toCHARGE is also a beautifully designed object—it looks just like a smooth pebble. It's available in several colors, as are the Bluetooth headphones from this Danish brand with its minimalist style I love so much.
The note: "To be forever connected"
kreafunk.com

MOVIES TO FALL IN LOVE TO

BRINGING UP BABY

Howard Hawks (1938)
Starring Katharine Hepburn
and Cary Grant
The famous line:
"There are only two things
I have to do: finish my brontosaurus
and get married at three o'clock."

HEAVEN CAN WAIT

Ernst Lubitsch (1943)
Starring Gene Tierney and Don Ameche
The famous line:
"The likelihood of one individual being
right increases in direct proportion
to the intensity with which others
are trying to prove him wrong."

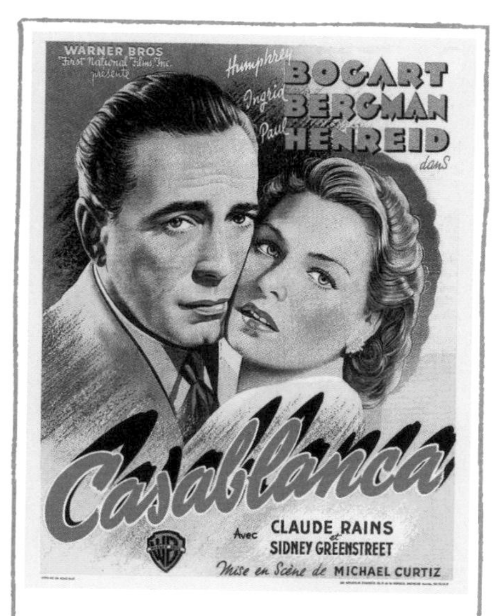

CASABLANCA

Michael Curtiz (1942)
Starring Humphrey Bogart
and Ingrid Bergman
The famous line:
"We'll always have Paris!"
and "Was that cannon fire,
or is it my heart pounding?"

HOW TO MARRY A MILLIONAIRE

Jean Negulesco (1953)
Starring Marilyn Monroe
and Lauren Bacall
The famous line:
"Most women use more brains picking
a horse in the third at Belmont than
they do picking a husband."

SOME LIKE IT HOT

Billy Wilder (1959)
Starring Marilyn Monroe and Tony Curtis
The famous line:
"Men who wear glasses are so much
more gentle, and sweet, and helpless."

THE APARTMENT

Billy Wilder (1960)
Starring Shirley MacLaine
and Jack Lemmon
The famous line:
"How could I be so stupid. You would think I should have learned by now. When you're in love with a married man you shouldn't wear mascara."

BREAKFAST AT TIFFANY'S

Blake Edwards (1961)
Starring Audrey Hepburn
The famous line:
"Be anything but a coward, a pretender, an emotional crook. . . : I'd rather have cancer than a dishonest heart."

CHARADE

Stanley Donen (1963)
Starring Cary Grant and
Audrey Hepburn
The famous line:
"I don't bite, you know. . . .
Unless it's called for."

WHEN HARRY MET SALLY

Rob Reiner (1989)
Starring Meg Ryan and Billy Crystal
The famous line:
"I came here tonight because when you realize you want to spend the rest of your life with somebody, you want the rest of your life to start as soon as possible."

THE HOLIDAY

Nancy Meyers (2006)
Starring Cameron Diaz and Kate Winslet
The famous line:
"I suppose I think about love
more than anyone ever should.
I'm constantly amazed by its sheer
power to alter and define our lives."

FORREST GUMP

Robert Zemeckis (1994)
Starring Tom Hanks and
Robin Wright Penn
The famous line:
"Jenny and me was like peas and carrots."

Romantic tunes

"When a Man Loves a Woman"
Percy Sledge (1966)
This is the first love song that comes to mind.
Partly because of the title, but also because we slow danced
to it as teenagers (along with Otis Redding's
"That's How Strong My Love Is"—see below),
and we take songs seriously at that age.

"And It's Supposed to Be Love"
Ayo (2006)
I love Ayo's sexy voice and the ambience
this song creates. It's the perfect tune
to listen to on your way to a first date,
to get you in the mood.

"Thinking Out Loud"
Ed Sheeran (2014)
For many people, the quintessential love song is Edith Piaf's
"Hymne à L'Amour." But I'd like to make a break
with tradition by proposing something more contemporary,
like this one. Love songs don't have to be from ancient history!

"Tes tendres années" (Your tender years)

Johnny Hallyday (1963)

This is the ultimate love song. It's about a man who loves a woman who loves another man, but his love is unconditional. When Johnny died, no one mentioned this track. But of all his music, I like this one best—and it's one of my favorite songs of all time.

❤

"L'Appuntamento"

Ornella Vanoni (1970)

In this song, which featured on the soundtrack for the movie *Ocean's Twelve*, Ornella confesses she's made mistakes in love so many times, and is well aware she's most likely making another one today—but hey, that's the miracle of love! A classic Italian pop song.

❤

"That's How Strong My Love Is"

Otis Redding (1965)

I can't make a playlist without including Otis Redding. I've been listening to his music since I was thirteen. I'm torn between this one and "I've Been Loving You Too Long."

❤

"Marry You"

Bruno Mars (2011)

He thinks he wants to marry her! This one is crystal clear—-and practical for shy types who are having trouble plucking up the courage to propose. Play the song and find out if the answer is yes . . . or no.

❤

"I Love You"

Frank Sinatra

(1962)

I'd love to hear someone say I'm just too good to be true. . . . Wouldn't you?

"Happiness is contagious. Children experience delight when they are raised in a happy environment. If your children's well-being is important to you, work on being happy yourself."

—Boris Cyrulnik

It's a FAMILY AFFAIR

The traditional family unit has evolved enormously over the past decades, but its importance remains the same: our family provides us with support and a sense of solidarity, as well as unconditional love. It is an essential source of the happiness that we carry with us our entire life.

So, if you want a wonderful family, you have to stop and consider your own childhood: what are you comfortable with and what do you refuse to repeat? Failing to engage in this kind of reflection can have negative consequences for the rest of your life. Analyze your experience without making judgment.

You become an adult when you can forgive your parents and don't try to change them.

Also accept the fact that in some ways you are like your parents, while keeping in mind that you have your own story and genetic makeup. Often, this requires trying to understand why you react the way you do. There's always a reason, and if you know what it is, you can easily tone things down. Why don't you like celebrating birthdays? Maybe because your parents never celebrated yours.

Bringing up BABY

If you have children, pay attention to what neuroscientists have discovered.

The empathy and kindness parents show toward their children contribute to healthy brain development.

Once you understand this, the work of educating a child (yes, it takes a little work) becomes much easier—and effective.

Who decided that kindness is corny and only for the weak?

Today, I'm marching (in a pink vest) for a return to kindness.

Parents, rise up— and be nice!

MY RECIPE FOR RAISING HAPPY KIDS

TRUST: THE FOUNDATION FOR RAISING CHILDREN. There's a bad combination that leaves parents with a bitter taste in their mouths: not trusting their children and giving in to fear. Children raised that way are going to get caught up in conflicts for no real reason.

LOTS OF KISSES FROM THE MOMENT THEY'RE BORN. Holding them is also highly recommended. And don't hesitate to walk around with baby strapped in the carrier like a little kangaroo while you clean or work during naptime. This practice is backed up by many studies recommending the **Kangaroo Method** for premature babies.

WHAT IS IT? Give babies skin-to-skin time with their parents. This method has been shown to reduce infant mortality, serious illness, infections, and hospitalizations. It also helps babies sleep longer. Developed in Columbia in 1978 to compensate for a lack of incubators for premature babies, the method proves that affection and touch contribute significantly to a child's well-being.

TAKING THINGS ***TOO SERIOUSLY***
MAKES FOR A REALLY
UNHAPPY LIFE.

JANET GIBSON, professor of cognitive psychology at Grinnell College in Iowa, explains in an article published in *The Conversation* that humor is a sign of good mental health. And if you have a sense of humor, you should share it with others because it also contributes to their well-being, by reducing stress and strengthening bonds.

Remember: making people laugh shouldn't be taken lightly—it's a serious business!

MAINTAINING COMMUNICATION.

Talking to your kids is also crucial to raising them well, especially when it comes to "sensitive" subjects.

GONE ARE THE DAYS WHEN PARENTS AVOIDED TALKING ABOUT DRUGS, ALCOHOL, ETC. *Your objective:* to make your child feel protected and equipped to confront any risk. The real danger lies in not talking to your kids—they have to be prepared for anything.

Explain the many possible ways to get out of a tricky situation. Tell them that they shouldn't be afraid to duck into a store for help if a strange adult follows them. I'm always shocked to see that certain subjects are still taboo, even for twenty-first-century parents. Kids won't wait for you to give them the information they want; so you may as well explain your point of view and how you would extricate yourself from a problem situation.

TO MAINTAIN COMMUNICATION WITH YOUR KIDS, *try to keep meals at the table, without the presence of the TV or smartphones.* This may seem *obvious*, but I know many parents who *never* eat lunch or dinner with their children. That's a shame.

For a long time, the saying went, "The quality of time spent with your kids is more important than the quantity." True, but I think you also have to put in the quantity. Kids need time to tell you what's going on in their lives.

NEVER FORGET THAT YOU ARE AN EXAMPLE FOR YOUR CHILDREN!

If you're quick to anger, spit insults, or fly into a rage,
don't be surprised if your kids do the same.
Aggressiveness has never been a recommended form of discipline.

I don't think I'm going out on a limb when I say that.

4 "rules" FOR WELL-ROUNDED KIDS

1
Follow a
ROUTINE

When children are young, I think it's necessary to have a somewhat regular schedule, especially when it comes to sleep. How many times have I heard teachers at parent meetings say, "Try to get your kids to bed early. The school desk is not the best place to make up for lost sleep." But don't skimp on bedtime stories: they support your child's developing brain. And that's been scientifically proven.

2
Write
LEGIBLY

First, because not everyone has a degree in hieroglyphics or the skills to decode sloppy handwriting. And also because teachers just don't have the time to try and decipher homework before correcting it.

3
Brush
YOUR TEETH

AND

wash
EVERY DAY

4
Learn good
TABLE MANNERS

Don't hold your fork like a tennis racket and don't talk with your mouth full—it inhibits proper digestion.

CHILDREN NEED *REGULARITY* TO FEEL *SECURE.*

What don't they need?

EXCESSIVE authority.

Being strict won't get you far, and neither will banning your children from doing something. When you tell kids not to eat candy, they'll find a way to eat it at some point—and probably a lot more than if you had just given them a little yourself.

Kids want what they can't have.

Establishing a routine also means you can break it sometimes to do unexpected things, like going out into the street at night after a snowstorm or picnicking in the bedroom instead of eating at the dinner table.

REMEMBER: YOUR CHILDREN DON'T BELONG TO YOU!

I've always thought that having children is a miracle (and mine truly are because I had a hard time getting pregnant). And I've also realized that they are not our private property. Yes, we are responsible for our children, but they are individuals who will one day do just fine without us. For that reason, we have to accept that we can't control everything and that not everything depends on us. Early on, we have to accept the fact that we are not the center of their world. Our job is to help them become independent.

Of course, I could criticize many things about the way I raised my children. There were times when I traveled *a lot*. I told myself, "It's only four days away from them, it's not that long." But for them, four days was an eternity.

I always want to look on the bright side, so I try to put everything into perspective. But this philosophy can be irritating. *I know this full well.*

We need to accept that no one is perfect.

TEENS ARE *EASY!*

What if teenage meltdowns were caused by parents who can't stand to see their babies grow up? It's a period of change—*that ends.* During this phase, which can last from the age of twelve to eighteen, or longer, it's important to remember that using humiliation as a disciplinary tactic is the worst possible strategy. You'll get better results by talking with your kids than by confronting them, especially while they're in this "rebellious" period. *Your mission is to defuse tension!*

PEACEFUL PARENT-TEENAGER RELATIONS

Don't get *unreasonably angry.*

Don't cut off communication over *small disputes.*

Your teenager has left a can of soda in the living room or clothes on the bedroom floor. There's no point in grounding them for a week to prevent it from happening again. That would be totally unreasonable. Stupid, even. You would lose your *credibility as a parent.* Parents must learn self-control and discernment. Before flying into a rage over a pair of underpants forgotten on the floor, ask yourself, "What would the Dalai Lama do?"

If you break off communication, you break your *connection.* Kids have to be able to tell us everything that's bothering them. They should know that we're always there for them, even if sometimes they prefer to talk about their problems with friends. In any case, just because one of them forgot to take out the trash, there is no reason to be difficult. When you live with teenagers, putting yourself in the shoes of a Buddhist monk is the solution to every "problem."

SIX THINGS YOU SHOULD NEVER DO TO A TEENAGER:

- Fail to *immediately* wash the sweatshirt they put in the dirty laundry bin last night. Expect to get your head bitten off.

- Ask your eighteen-year-old if they plan to eat at home. You'll be declared a *dictator*.

- Establish a curfew. You'll be accused of *blackmail*.

- Say anything *slightly negative* about their girl-/boyfriend. You'll immediately be called an *old grinch*.

- Mention that your teen's friend's eyeliner looks gothic. You'll be labeled a *has-been*.

- Invite them on vacation *without their friends*. They'll just go ahead and prove they can get themselves invited on vacation *without you*.

3 COMPLETELY RIDICULOUS THINGS THAT SOME PARENTS SAY:

"I got a few wallops and it didn't kill me."

"We're going away, just the two of us. We'll get some peace without the kids around!"

"DON'T BE CHILDISH!"

HOW TO AVOID MAKING A MISSTEP IN A STEPFAMILY

The role of stepmother or stepfather is certainly one of the hardest to play in a blended family. It's important to remember that a stepparent has duties but no rights. The role is complex: you can give advice (which won't always be taken), but you must never be authoritarian. Above all, don't try to be a stand-in for mom or dad. Basically, it requires taking a giant step back. Maintaining a certain distance from the situation will show that you've understood what it means to be a stepparent.

Don't forget that even though divorce is very common, it is never inconsequential. I'm not questioning divorce, but I think you have to bear in mind that it isn't easy for children. No longer having both of their parents under the same roof, when that's all they've ever known, is extremely unsettling for them. And even if everything seems to be going well when they're young, wounds can emerge later. That's why stepparents must learn how to smooth relationships that could sour quickly.

• THESE WORDS SET ME **FREE** •

It goes for fathers, too

Stop thinking you can control everything.

We live with our baggage,
so be natural and you will be
the best parent in the world
to your children.

PUPPY LOVE

I can't talk about family without mentioning **dogs**. They're a big part of my life. When I was a young model, I took my dog **Jim** everywhere with me. He even had a portfolio full of photos of himself. Dogs have genuine medical usefulness: they act as an antidepressant. When you pet a dog, your body secretes **oxytocin**, the "love hormone." Apparently, owning a dog also slows aging. It makes sense: you walk him, throw him a ball, and go out to buy him food. And let's not forget all the studies that prove that spending time with dogs lowers blood pressure and **protects** us from cardiovascular disease.

In other words,
our friends bring us happiness,
but so does our dog.
(Much the same can be said
for your cat, rabbit, fish, etc.,
if you're not a dog person.)

WHY ARE DOGS SO GREAT?

They have far fewer side effects
than antidepressants.

They always agree with you.

If you're single, they may lead you to meet
the love of your life—think of the movie *101 Dalmatians*.

Some dogs can also be bodyguards.
But not all of them: Dinky,
our Bichon Maltese, is not very effective!

→ *Family* IS THE GREATEST GIFT

"The best gift I could ever have is you—my family!"
That's often the reply when a family member asks what we'd like for our birthday or Christmas. But hey, presents are nice too.

Skin Tea Molecular Herbal Infusion by Dr. Barbara Sturm:
for your loved ones' well-being
What could be more thoughtful than protecting the health of those you love? This tisane, with chamomile, ginger, fennel, licorice, and pink rose petals, is soothing and relaxing. A delicious herbal tea in an attractive jar—everything feels good thanks to this magic potion.
drsturm.com

A cooking class:
to spend quality time together
Creating something together always strengthens bonds. Whether it be a cake or some other creation, the important thing is to enjoy the activity together as a family. To learn how to make delicious croissants or macarons *à la française*, sign the family up for an online class in English on
lacuisineparis.teachable.com

An exhibition ticket or a museum membership:
to improve your knowledge as a family
I could invite my family to spend the day shopping at the mall, but I like the idea of them learning something. A trip to a museum or gallery might be met with cries of disapproval from teenagers glued to Instagram and TikTok, but it is my duty to send them out into the Metaverse armed with cultural knowledge.

Blank Slate: The Game Where ___ Minds Think Alike:
to see how well you really know each other
In our increasingly virtual world, board games are the perfect solution to bring us together. The object of this amusing game is to complete the phrase on one of the word cue cards, while trying to match just one other player's word. Those who know each other the best will be the winners!
theop.games

FAMILY MOVIES & SERIES...

... TO HELP YOU RELATE TO YOUR TEENAGER

FERRIS BUELLER'S DAY OFF

John Hughes (1986)
"How can I possibly be expected to handle school on a day like this?" That's the sentence that justifies the whole film. A teenage boy decides to play hooky and drive around town with his friends in the sunshine. And so the adventure begins. Of course, you don't need to be a teen to sometimes want to skip work and take a long stroll instead.
The famous line:
"You can never go too far."

CLUELESS

Amy Heckerling
(1995)
A classic. The famous closet of Cher Horowitz, a high-school student in Beverly Hills, has become iconic, along with her yellow plaid mini-skirt. This is the movie that perfectly encapsulates teenage dramas.
The famous line:
"Old people can be so sweet."

SEX EDUCATION

Kate Herron and Ben Taylor
(2019)
A TV series for the new generation that revolves around sex. Teen Otis Milburn, whose mother is a sex therapist, sets up a sex therapy clinic at school. It's perfect for broaching tricky subjects with your teen.
The famous line:
"You can't choose who you're attracted to. You can't engineer a relationship."

... TO ENJOY WITH THE LITTLE ONES

BAMBI

Walt Disney
(1942)
A classic animated film featuring the cutest characters.
Even though the young fawn experiences a tragedy,
this movie, which recounts Bambi's early years
in the forest, still fills me with wonder. I adore fawns
and does, so this cartoon was bound to be my favorite.
The famous line:
"If you can't say something nice, don't say nothing at all."

RATATOUILLE

Pixar
(2007)
Who wouldn't want to live in the Paris
portrayed in this animated film?
Remy's charm is enough to reconcile us with
rats—quite useful when you live in Paris.
The famous line:
"Anyone can cook, but only the fearless
can be great."

... TO MAKE YOU FEEL NOSTALGIC

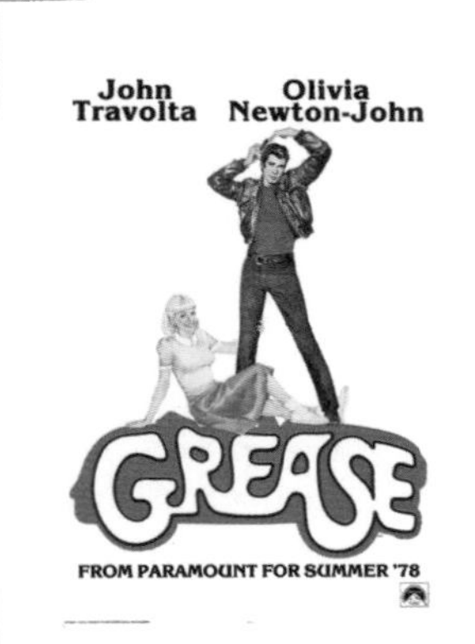

GREASE

Randal Kleiser
(1978)
This musical tells the tale of
a high-school girl in the 1950s.
Starring Olivia Newton-John and
John Travolta, who embodies the era's
rock'n'roll spirit, this film is iconic.
The famous line:
"The rules are . . . there ain't no rules!"

Family tunes

"We Are Family"
Sister Sledge (1979)
This song seems a logical choice, since the group was composed of four sisters. Today, it also springs to mind when we want to talk about solidarity between people. I don't have any sisters, but I do have plenty of friends whom I consider family—so I can sing this song with them!

♬

"Isn't She Lovely"
Stevie Wonder (1976)
Stevie Wonder composed this song to celebrate his daughter Aisha's birth. I don't have any song-writing talent, but I would've loved to write a song like this one for my daughters.

♬

"Celebration"
Kool and the Gang (1980)
When organizing a family gathering, it is essential to think about the ambience. "Celebration" is a party tune that's full of energy and sets the tone for a great evening ahead. Try to talk about touchy subjects with this song playing—it's impossible!

♬

"Cover Me in Sunshine"
Pink & Willow Sage Hart (2021)
This song is a true family affair, since Pink sings it with her ten-year-old daughter. It's lovely to share your passion with your children. Pink once confessed that singing this song at home with her kids made her so happy. It's a tune to hum to your heart's content.

"Success is the ability to go from one failure to another with no loss of enthusiasm."

—Winston Churchill

BUSINESS as USUAL

Workplace
happiness !

Olga and I work together every day, so I figured we were going to come up with all kinds of tips for a successful and joyful day at work.

BUT ULTIMATELY,

I don't think there's a handbook for how to achieve a happy and fulfilling professional life.

Perhaps the most important thing is to turn your passion into your profession. We spend such a huge part of our lives at work, so it's important to love what we do and to get on with those we work with. A study by the University of Warwick revealed that contented workers are up to 12 percent more productive than their unhappy counterparts. Workplace happiness has positive repercussions on health and even personal relationships, as well as being crucial for motivation at work.

I like to quote something

Steve Jobs,

cofounder of Apple, said during a speech he gave at Stanford in 2005:

"Sometimes life hits you in the head with a brick. Don't lose faith. I'm convinced that the only thing that kept me going was that I loved what I did.... [T]he only way to be truly satisfied is to do what you believe is great work. And the only way to do great work is to love what you do. And if you haven't found it yet, keep looking. Don't settle. As with all matters of the heart, you'll know when you find it. And, like any great relationship, it just gets better and better as the years roll on."

MAKE A LIST OF EVERYTHING YOU *LIKE* AND *DISLIKE* ABOUT YOUR CURRENT JOB

If the latter outweighs the former, perhaps it's time for a change. Note down your passions and the careers that could match. My advice to those who are unsure of which path to take is to choose a profession that you'd gladly do for free.

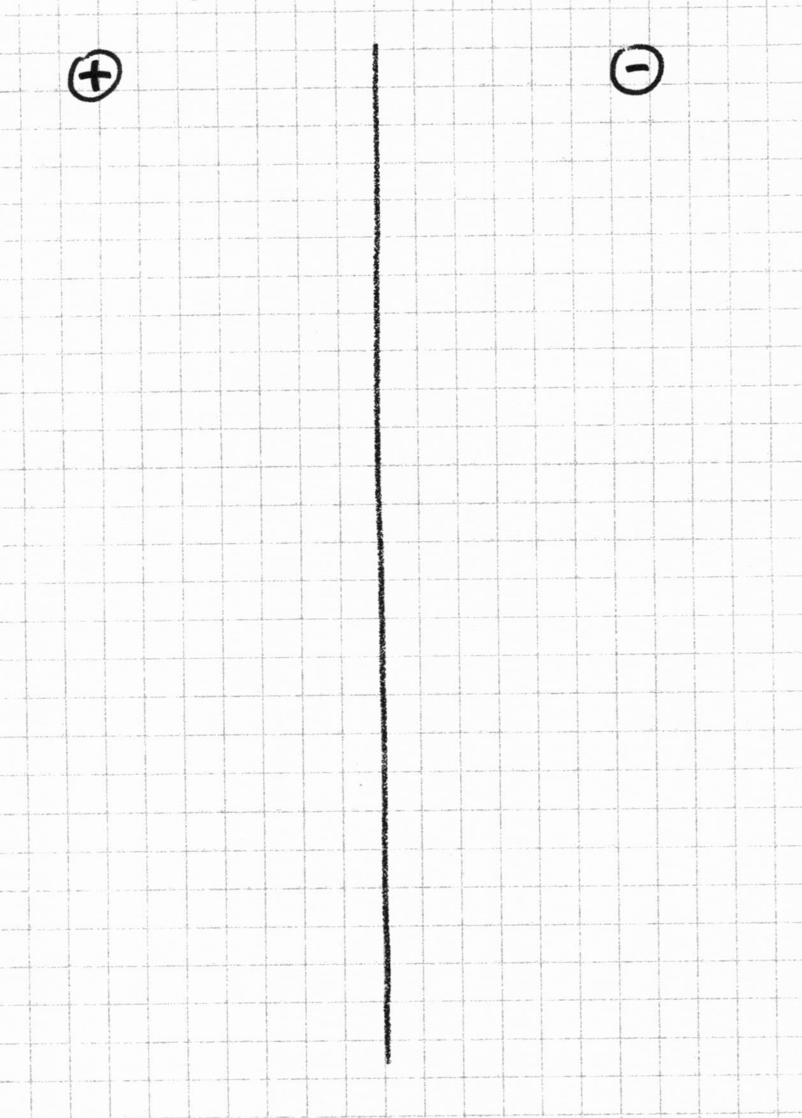

THE ONLY SKILL THAT SHOULD BE REQUIRED FOR ANY JOB:

KNOWING HOW TO REMOVE YOURSELF FROM DRAMA AT WORK

It seems that some people delight in bad news: they turn everything into an epic disaster and imagine the smallest things bringing ruin to the company. This perpetually frazzled colleague doesn't seem to realize how fortunate they actually are. "The delivery didn't arrive today—what a catastrophe!" complains a distraught colleague to occupy their morning. Unless someone's life is in danger, the situation is not that serious. It can take years, but sometimes you can make these people understand that drama is pointless. Often, it just means realizing that things can take a little more time than we expected; keeping that in mind can make all the difference.

Roger Vivier
PARIS
BERGDORF
GOODMAN

IT'S NEW!

ACE YOUR NEXT VIDEOCONFERENCE

IT'S NEW!

THE PANDEMIC forced us to work remotely and start videoconferencing. No one looks good on a computer or telephone screen—whether you're a model or not. Now I understand why certain apps come with filters. To avoid appearing in all your videoconferences with a cat's head hiding your own, I asked my friend **LYDIA PUJOLS** for some tips. She's been my makeup artist forever and works on a lot of film shoots—so she knows how to apply makeup to get beautiful onscreen results.

AND THEY CAN APPLY TO MEN TOO.

Well, perhaps not all of them, but a little concealer can make you look more efficient in the eyes of your coworkers.

LYDIA'S *advice*

LIGHTING IS IMPORTANT

Position lighting elements in line with your face to soften shadows. Choose a white light—a LED lamp works well—and add a second light source in the background.

HIGH DEFINITION MAKEUP

You want to soften volume and color contrasts. Even out your complexion with a light liquid foundation or a BB cream to make your skin look bright and clear. Apply an orange color correcting concealer to minimize under-eye circles and a green color correcting concealer to hide redness. If you have beautiful, even skin tone, you can forget the foundation; a touch of under-eye concealer is enough to neutralize shadows and brighten your complexion.

I ALSO LIKE TO REDEFINE THE EYEBROWS

Build up density using a pencil or powder to fill in any gaps. You don't want to harden your expression; you want to add character to your eyes.

Once you've achieved even skin tone, you can use:

PINK CREAM BLUSH
for a touch of freshness or bronze blush to create
the illusion that you've been lounging in the sun.

AN EYELASH CURLER
and mascara to open up the eye area
(and make you look more awake!).

A brown, black, russet, or navy blue
EYELINER PENCIL
to draw a line across your upper eyelid, up and out,
from inner to outer edge.

NEUTRAL OR PALE LIPSTICK.
Avoid dark colors; go for natural-looking lips.

And don't forget to:

Use a clean and tidy background. **KEEP IT SIMPLE**,
and make sure there's nothing distracting or unsightly
in view (put that laundry away).

Choose a **QUIET LOCATION**, where you won't be disturbed.
Screaming kids bursting into the room
will not enhance your professional image.

Find a **FLATTERING CAMERA ANGLE**. Your colleagues don't
want to see up your nostrils. And you risk causing a crick
in your neck if you position the camera too high—
ensure it is placed at eye level.

TEST THE VIDEO CONFERENCE LINK beforehand
and get all your documents ready in advance.

MOVIES & SERIES
THAT DO THE JOB

WORKING GIRL

Mike Nichols
(1988)
One of the first films to spotlight the hurdles encountered by women during their careers. In this movie, a secretary, who is badly treated in her first job, then has her idea stolen by her boss.
It has become a cult movie that also offers insight into the concept of "power dressing."
The famous line:
"I have a head for business and a body for sin. Is there anything wrong with that?"

GIRLBOSS

Kay Cannon (2017)
Inspired by the partially autobiographical novel *#GIRLBOSS* by Sophia Amoruso, this TV series recounts the life of a girl who likes buying vintage clothing and ends up starting a business from her passion. I love the idea that a passion can turn into a job.
The famous line:
"No matter where you are in life, you'll save a lot of time by not worrying too much about what other people think about you. The earlier in your life that you can learn that, the easier the rest of it will be."

SUITS

Aaron Korsh (2011)
This series (all nine seasons) takes place in a New York City law firm. It's a great way to familiarize yourself with the legal world. And to check out if Meghan Markle, who plays a paralegal, is a convincing actor.
The famous line:
"I don't have dreams, I have goals."

THE INTERN

Nancy Meyers (2015)
The main character in this film is a seventy-year-old intern working at a start-up, which inevitably results in hilarious situations. It also makes you think about the fact that age is actually only a number and that mixing experienced people with rookies can in fact lead to great achievements.
The famous line:
"It's 2015, are we really still critical of working moms?"

THE DEVIL WEARS PRADA

David Frankel (2006)
Based on Lauren Weisberger's novel of the same name, this movie is always mentioned when talking about the world of fashion. Considering my involvement in the fashion business, I couldn't possibly overlook this film, but I am certain that fashion magazine assistants are not all treated like that—it's fiction, after all!
The famous line:
"You sold your soul to the devil when you put on your first pair of Jimmy Choo's, I saw it."

FEEL-GOOD *tunes* TO START THE *working day*

"River Deep Mountain High"
Ike & Tina Turner (1966)
This always takes me back to my childhood; my parents listened to this when we lived in the countryside. Simon & Garfunkel's "Mrs. Robinson" (1968) has the same effect, too.

♫

"Maybellene"
Chuck Berry (1956)
This also brings back memories! When I was fifteen, I met Mick Jagger. He asked me what kind of music I listened to. I said, "Chuck Berry." He approved, but then he asked me, "Do you listen to the Stones?" I said, "Yes." Then he asked me what song. Confused and intimidated, I replied, "Lady Jane." And he told me that was a very good choice too, because it was inspired by Irish folklore. Still, it wasn't exactly representative of their music!

"Dead Flowers"
The Rolling Stones (1971)
This one immediately puts me in a good mood. I heartily recommend listening to it in the morning, just after waking up. It's the perfect song to get dressed to!

♫

"You Send Me"
Aretha Franklin (1957)
I can't forget Aretha, any more than I can Janis Joplin, Amy Winehouse, and Barbara.

♫

"S.O.B"
Nathaniel Rateliff & The Night Sweats (2015)
Play this at the office in the middle of the afternoon and you'll set the place on fire.

♫

"La Terre est ronde"
(The Earth is round)
Orelsan (2015)
I really like Orelsan's sharp lyrics.

♫

"Bonne bonne humeur ce matin"
(Good good mood this morning)
Tristan (1988)
Sing and dance yourself into a good mood with this one. I had to include this song, not least because of the line about Paris being full, full, full of Parisians, not enough Parisian girls and too many Parisian guys!

"I wear my sort of clothes to save me the trouble of deciding which clothes to wear."

—Katharine Hepburn

STYLE for ALL

Our relationships with others are essential for our well-being, but, ultimately, happiness starts with us. We need to take care of ourselves. After all, there is truth in the old adage that when you look good, you feel good. And this, in turn, has a beneficial effect on our friends, family, and colleagues!

STYLE FOR OTHERS

Even though we mainly buy clothes because we like them, we still think about the impression they're going to make on others. One of my goals is to bring a little joy into my life—and the life of those around me—with looks that aren't too dull. And to women who have grown too accustomed to the easiness of wearing black, I gently explain that color is important for morale. The expression "put a little color into your life" should be taken literally.

20 pieces TO BRIGHTEN UP *your life* (AND EVERYONE ELSE'S)

→ *Each has a purpose*

THE FUCHSIA CARDIGAN

"I'm in a good mood."

YELLOW SNEAKERS

"We're at the beach!"

PATTERNED CARDIGANS

"Keeping warm Scandi-style."

NEON SWEATERS

"I'm pretty bright."

RED PANTIES

"A lucky charm in Italy."

GOLD BALLERINA FLATS

"Every day is Christmas."

GOLD SANDALS
"I love to shine."

PRINTED SCARVES
"Details are never accessory."

A PINK SWEATER
"I've decided to see la vie en rose.*"*

SOMETHING IN KHAKI
"Khaki is a happy version of black."

RED BOOTS
"Burning down the house."

A GOLD SEQUIN BAG
"I want sparkle in my life."

A RED CLUTCH
"Adds a dose of energy to any look."

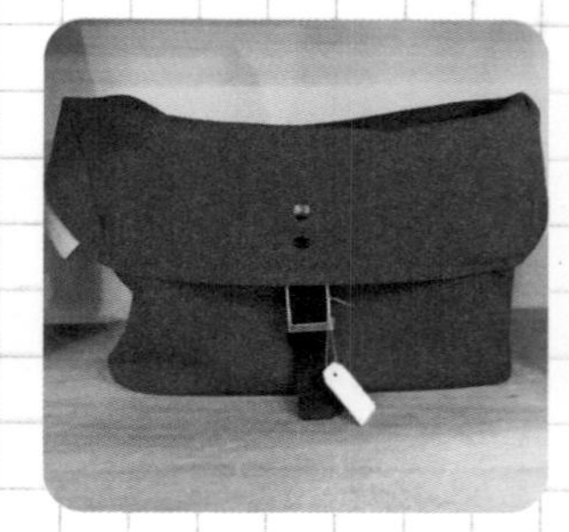

A BLUE MESSENGER BAG
"Nothing but blue skies."

A WHITE SHIRT
"Snow white."

A TINY GLITTERY BAG
"A glowing evening in store."

A RED SWEATER
"Objective: flamboyance."

A GREEN PANTSUIT
"This outfit gets the green light."

A COLORFUL PLAID SHIRT
"Even if you're square, you can be cheerful."

A YELLOW JACKET
"Here comes the sun!"

3 LOOKS THAT WILL PUT EVERYONE *in a good mood*

A LIGHT PINK SWEATER + *jeans*

Ok, even if I just proved to you that my closet holds much more than *navy blue sweaters and raw denim jeans*, I can't deny it—this duo is a big part of my wardrobe. And I have enough for all of my friends!

PINK SWEATER
+
yellow skirt
+
PINK MOROCCAN BABOUCHE FLATS

WHITE PANTS
+
blue jacket
+
YELLOW CONVERSE SNEAKERS

GIVING

No guide to togetherness would be complete without mentioning donations. I go through phases with certain clothes (if you don't count white or raw denim jeans, white shirts, and navy blue sweaters), and when I'm done wearing them, I don't sell them through a secondhand fashion app (although that's a great idea, too)—I give them away. And when one of my friends says she likes something I'm wearing, my reflex is to give it to her right away. While writing this chapter, Olga and Sophie, my coauthors, confessed that, although they always love how I'm dressed, they don't tell me anymore because they're afraid I'll end up naked.

WHERE CAN I MAKE DONATIONS?

There are plenty of options: city halls, places of worship, and schools will likely have a list of places where you can donate your clothes. Here are some international organizations:

- **The American Red Cross**, *redcross.org*
- **Goodwill**, *goodwill.org*
- **The Salvation Army**, *salvationarmy.org*
- **Oxfam International**, *oxfam.org*

If you have professional clothing like pantsuits and blazers, consider donating them to the non-profit **Dress for Success** (dressforsuccess.org), which is present in 25 countries. The organization provides low-income women with work-appropriate clothing as they seek and maintain employment.

A SECOND LIFE FOR ORPHAN SOCKS

I've never understood how I lose so many socks. I have a bag of lone socks that went into the machine as a pair but came out single. Luckily the people at **Chaussettes Orphelines** (en.chaussettesorphelines.com) have studied this global issue. The organization recycles socks to make new garments such as hats, gloves, scarves, and even bags.

GIVING AND RECYCLING IS A FASHIONABLE NEW COMBINATION!

Marius

Body positivity
AND TOGETHERNESS

When it comes to beauty and health, I could give you a whole program featuring a complete skin care routine, balanced diet, and exercise classes to sculpt your body—but that's not like me at all! People often ask me, "What do you do to stay so thin?" Not much, really; I just try to eat slowly and stop when I'm not hungry anymore. But there's something else: you shouldn't compare your body to other people's. That also makes it easier to live in a community. The growing "body positivity" movement is absolutely necessary. Everyone should be proud of their body—that's what fuels personal style and makes you a centerpiece among others. Even though I'm getting older (and fatter), I "positivize" my body. And I don't talk about aging much anymore. But I'm happier today than I was at twenty. I'd even go so far as to say that you only learn what happiness really is at fifty. Sleep and laughter are definitely the best secrets to staying young—and to laugh, you need friends!

"Good food is the foundation of genuine happiness."

—Auguste Escoffier

AROUND the TABLE

It will come as no surprise

to hear that there is an inextricable link between food and happiness. Eating is one of life's great pleasures, and we all have our favorite foods that bring instant gratification or that cheer us up when we're feeling down. Certain types of food can also have beneficial effects on our mood and behavior. And there is no better way to bring people together than through food: gathering around the table to share a meal keeps us all connected and, according to experts, can lead to a happier—and healthier—life.

What's the fastest way to make **FRIENDS?**

EAT THE SAME FOOD TOGETHER!

According to a 2016 study by the Society of Consumer Psychology, eating the same food helps establish a relationship of trust between strangers. Ayelet Fishbach, who coauthored the study, explains: "I think food is powerful because it is something that we put into our bodies and we need to trust it in order to do that. I hope our research will be used to connect people and facilitate conflict resolution."

Organize team lunches where everyone eats the same thing and you'll quickly see team members bonding.

SERVICES SECRETS
PICASSO

dure

GOOD TO KNOW:

I won't get into the technical details, but according to a study by the University of Lübeck in Germany, eating protein makes people more conciliatory. This is due to tyrosine: a molecule present in protein that stimulates production of dopamine, a neurotransmitter that influences the decision-making process. *The more dopamine we produce, the more tolerant we are.*

I was reluctant to reveal this information here—now my children will understand why I happily serve them an egg each morning.

I should tell you that I eat quinoa,
but I'm not going to lie to you!
One of my favorite feel-good foods is Marks & Spencer's
sweet-and-savory popcorn.

I can eat six bags in less
than thirty minutes!

THE ITALIAN COFFEE RITUAL

I would never think of badmouthing a certain coffee machine sold by a certain handsome man, but if you have the time, I highly recommend trying the **NEAPOLITAN COFFEE** ritual. Not only is it *beautiful,* it's also *very good.* Pure joy in a cup....

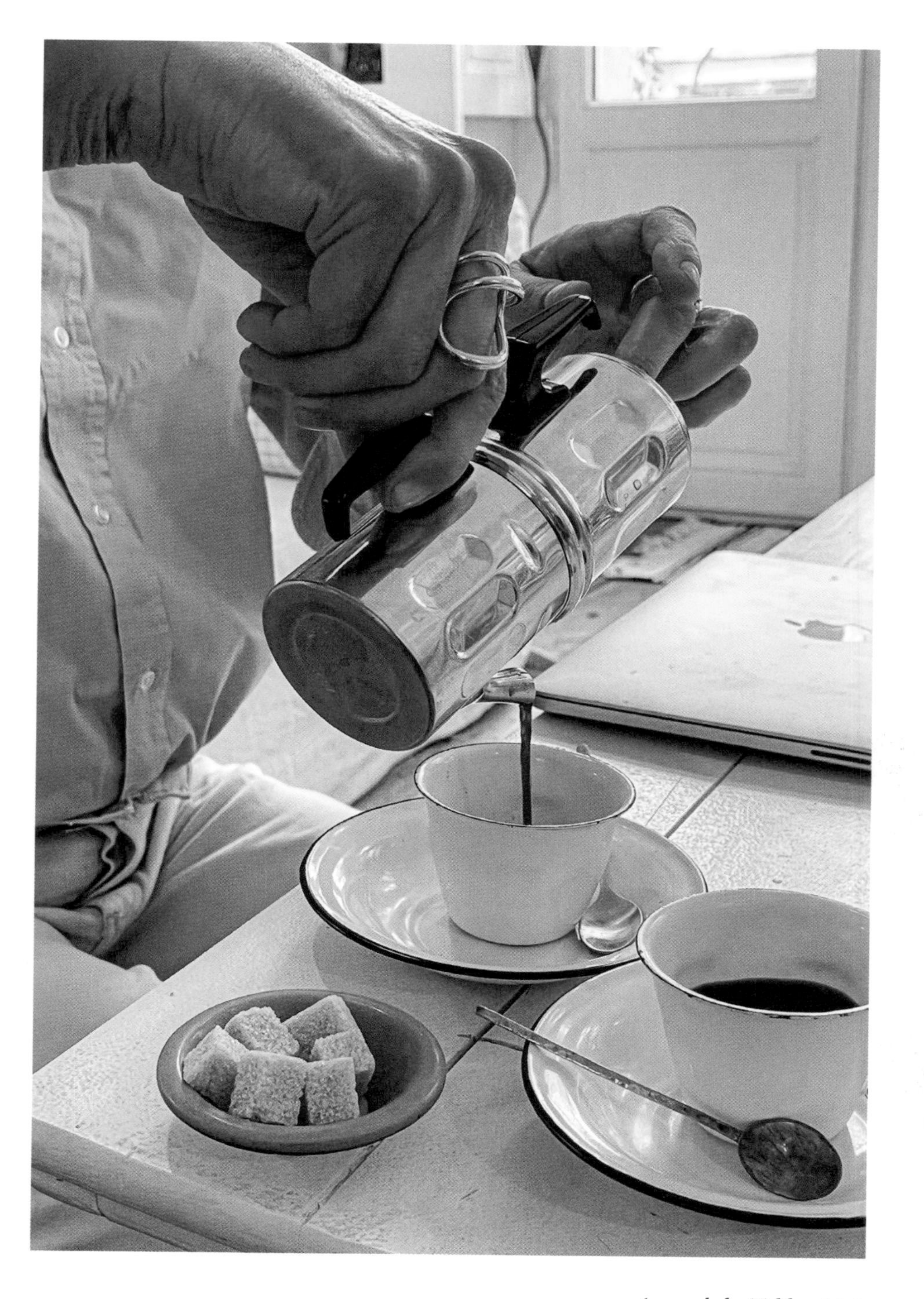

Conclusion
HAPPINESS Therapy

Our happiness depends on our perspective.

When you take care of yourself,
it's easier to take care of others.
Here are **15 SUGGESTIONS**
for a ***happier life***.

1

What if the solution was just deciding to be happy?

You can read all the personal development books you want, but nothing is more effective than unilateral action. *I decided long ago that I wanted nothing more than happiness.* Ok, so I may have taken some inspiration from Paul Éluard; he's my own personal source of positive affirmations. Remember: the best thing that ever happened to you was being born. It's a stroke of luck when you think of the minuscule odds you had of making it that far.

2

Make “to-do” lists

I like the idea of giving myself objectives; it makes me feel like I’m getting somewhere in life. Write down the things you need to do to succeed. *Be careful what you write, though: your plans could come to fruition more quickly than you think!*

Never scorn an activity

Running, walking, cooking, and cleaning are activities that give us time to think—and that could result in a *stroke of genius.*

Express gratitude

It’s easy to make a list of everything that’s going wrong, but realizing how lucky we are and making a list of the things we’re proud of—now that’s constructive. *And it will make you happy.*

5

Don't ever think yourself incapable

I wasn't selected at my first casting for Chanel because they said I was too tall. Well, after having been ambassador for the fashion house, I can tell you that first impressions are not always the best—you do have several chances to make a good first impression! *Never give up.*

Do whatever makes you happy!

That's always my reply when people ask me how to have a successful career. I've never done anything thinking, "What do I have to do to be successful?" Instead, I ask myself, "What would I like to wear, what do I need?" That's why I design navy blue blazers instead of neon pink crop tops. But luckily someone else designs neon pink crop tops!

7

Saying "I can do it" helps you reach your goal

But if you say, "I can't do it," you'll sink your ship. Saying "I'm thin," works too. But be careful: it isn't as effective if you eat three chocolate bars at once. These things have their limits.

Do less

I don't necessarily mean at work, where you probably shouldn't take it too easy if you want to keep your job. *But you should allow yourself to slow down* and while away the time. Even just ten minutes in bed. And don't forget to bring your sense of humor to work—if you're too serious, you'll feel like you're working too hard.

Let go

Need I say more? *Why kill yourself trying to make things perfect?* Just be aware of your limits and don't overdo it.

Learn to spot happiness

- A bouquet of daffodils bought on the way out of the subway.
- Stretching out on your bed after a bath.
- Coming home.
- Waking up ten minutes earlier to drink your tea in peace.

The little things are the foundation for great happiness.

11

Smile and life will smile back at you!

Ok, you're going to tell me that it isn't always so easy—*but it works.*

You're allowed to feel down

You don't have to follow a strict mantra of, "I'm ok, everything's ok." Of course, life has its difficult moments. I've certainly had my share. But there's no point in eternally dwelling on the problem, especially if you can't do anything about it, like grieving, for example. You're allowed to feel down and experience moments of vulnerability: *the important thing is to accept the situation* and confide in your friends to get through it. You see, even when giving personal development tips, it all comes back to togetherness!

13

Respect nature

Today, everyone should be aware of the pressing environmental issues, and *respecting the Earth makes you feel better.* Yes, recycling can lead to a certain form of nirvana.

Give and you shall receive

I admit, this one is obvious. But I still want to mention it, because when it comes to personal development, we sometimes forget that *helping and giving to others is necessary to maintain our own happiness.*

15

If you want to be happy, get some perspective

You have to practice at gaining perspective, because it doesn't come naturally. Remind yourself over and over, "It's not that serious, it doesn't matter." *You should always aim to take a step back* so you can see the bigger picture.

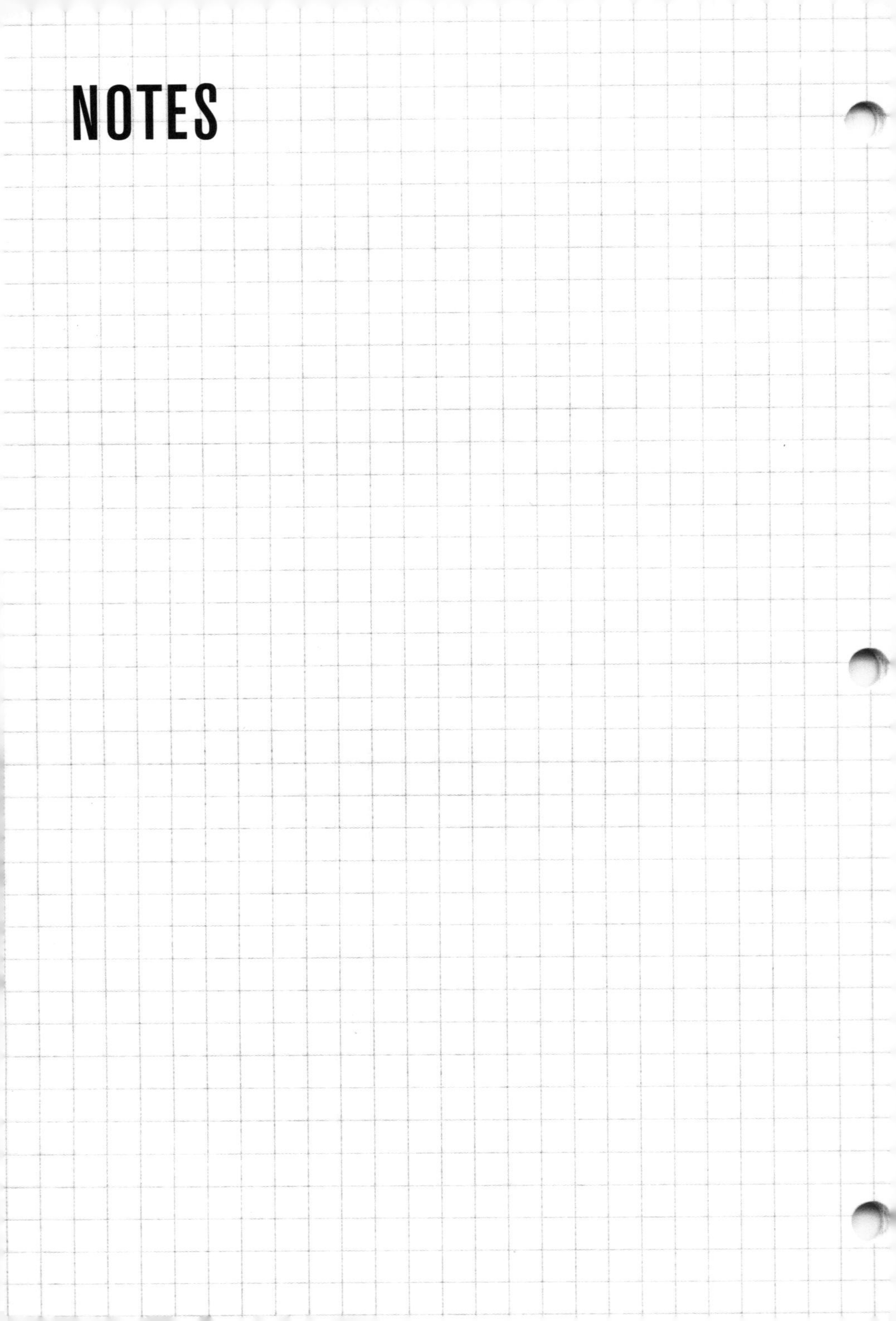
NOTES

Photographic Credits

All photographs by Olga Sekulic, with the exception of the following:
P. 37, from top to bottom: Vanessa Seward: © Jacqueline Burgalat; Guillaume Henry: © Damien Blottière; Marin Montagut: © Romain Ricard; Marie Hélène de Taillac: All Rights Reserved.
P. 38, from top to bottom: Pascale Monvoisin: All Rights Reserved; Isabelle Rosselini: © Paola Kudacki/Trunk Archive/photoSenso; Frédéric Perigot: © Jean Ber; Dominique Lionnet: All Rights Reserved.
P. 39, from top to bottom: Didier Papeloux: All Rights Reserved; Lilou Fogli: © Eddy Brière; Bertrand Burgalat: © Serge Leblon; Nicole Wisniak: © Richard Avedon.
P. 40, from top to bottom: Benedicte Perdriel: All Rights Reserved; Alexandre Mattiussi: © Luc Braquet; Bernard Chapuis: © Benoit Peverelli; Mireille Pellen: All Rights Reserved.
P. 41, from top to bottom: Lydia Pujols: All Rights Reserved; Boris Terral: All Rights Reserved; Héloïse Brion: © Christophe Roué; Charlotte Chesnais: All Rights Reserved.
P. 42, from top to bottom: Andrée Zana Murat: © Vincent Lappartient; Liya Kebede: All Rights Reserved; Gilles Bensimon: All Rights Reserved; Diego Della Valle: All Rights Reserved.
P. 43, from top to bottom: Elie Top: © Saskia Lawaks; Vincent Darré: All Rights Reserved; Delphine Courteille: All Rights Reserved.
P. 44, from top to bottom: Fifi Chachnil: © Roxane Moreau; Marie-France Cohen: All Rights Reserved; Cindy Bruna: © Sophie Gachet.
P. 46, left: Prod DB © RKO/All Rights Reserved; **right:** Prod DB © Amblin – Universal.
P. 47, top: Prod DB © MGM – Pathe Entertainment/All Rights Reserved; **bottom:** Prod DB © Warner/All Rights Reserved.
P. 48, top: Prod DB © 20th Century Fox/All Rights Reserved; **center:** Prod DB © Play Art – Filmsonor – Titanus; **bottom:** Prod DB © United Artists/All Rights Reserved.
P. 50: Prod DB © Warner Bros TV/All Rights Reserved.
P. 53: Warner Music.
P. 70, top: © 2020 by The Home Edit Print, LLC, published by Clarkson Potter, an imprint of Random House (Penguin Random House, LLC), cover photograph by Clea Shearer, book design by Mia Johnson; **bottom:** TableTopics® and the question mark pattern are registered trademarks of Ultra Pro International, LLC. All Rights Reserved.
P. 71, top: Polaroid Go®, © Polaroid; **center:** Power bank for cell phones by Kreafunk; **bottom:** © Swill Klitch/Shutterstock.
P. 72, left: Prod DB © RKO; **right:** Prod DB © 20th Century Fox/All Rights Reserved.
P. 73, top: Prod DB © Warner Bros/All Rights Reserved; **center:** Prod DB © 20th Century Fox; **bottom:** Prod DB © 20th Century Fox/All Rights Reserved.
P. 74, top: Collection Christophel © Mirisch Corporation; **center:** Prod DB © Paramount; **bottom:** Prod DB © Universal Pictures – Stanley Donen Films.
P. 75, top: Prod DB © Columbia Pictures – Castle Rock Entertainment – Nelson Entertainment; **center:** Prod DB © Universal / All Rights Reserved; **bottom:** Prod DB © Paramount.
P. 80: Dominique Charriau/WireImage/Getty Images.
P. 85: Bertrand Rindoff Petroff/Getty Images.
P. 94, top left: © Skin Tea Molecular Herbal Infusion by Dr. Barbara Sturm; **top right:** © David Franklin/123RF; **bottom right:** Invented by Bob Kamp, licensed and published by The Op Games – Usaopoly.
P. 95, top: © Paramount/Everett Collection/Aurimages; **bottom:** © Paramount Pictures/AF archive/Mary Evans/Aurimages.
P. 96: top: © Walt Disney/Everett Collection/Aurimages; **center**: © Disney/AF archive/Mary Evans/Aurimages; **bottom:** © Paramount/AF archive/Mary Evans/Aurimages.
P. 108: top: © Twentieth Century Fox/SunsetBox/AllPix/Aurimages; **bottom:** © Netflix/BBQ_DFY/Aurimages.
P. 109: top: © Hypnotic/Universal/AF archive/Mary Evans/Aurimages; **center:** © Waverly Films/Everett Collection/Aurimages; **bottom:** © Fox 2000/Dune Entertainment/Major Studio/Mary Evans/Aurimages.